LAND OF THE FREE
The U.S. Flag

Anne Hempstead

Heinemann Library
Chicago, Illinois

For more information address the publisher:
Raintree, 100 N. LaSalle, Suite 1200, Chicago IL 60602

Printed in China by WKT Company Limited

10 09 08 07 06
10 9 8 7 6 5 4 3 2 1

ISBN 1-4034-7002-2 (hc) -- ISBN 1-4034-7009-X (pb)

Library of Congress Cataloging-in-Publication Data:

Cataloging-in-publication data is on file at the Library of Congress.

Photo research by Julie Laffin

Acknowledgments
The author and publisher are grateful to the following for permission to reproduce copyright material:
p.4 Getty Images, pp. 7,9, 13, 16,24 The Granger Collection, p. 8 (a, b) Mary Evans Picture Library, pp.10, 26 Corbis/Bettmann, p.14 Smithsonian Institution, p.18 Library of Congress, p.20 © AP/Wide World Photos/Kathy Willens, p.22 © Donald Higgs.

Cover photo: © Getty Images/PhotoDisc

Contents

Chapter One: Broad Stripes and Bright Stars

The U.S. flag is one the nation's most beloved **symbols** of **democracy**. For many people around the world, the flag of the United States represents hope and justice.

The flag is a familiar part of everyday American life. People wave it at parades to celebrate that they are Americans. It hangs in classrooms, courtrooms, and many places of worship to honor the country's history and heroes. Americans proudly salute it at ballgames and public events. It flies over the U.S. Capitol, the White House, and most government buildings to represent the U.S. government—a government in which the people choose their own leaders.

The U.S. flag is easily recognized by its bold design of "broad stripes and bright stars." But the flag we know today is very different from the one that flew over the new **republic** in 1776. This is the story of how the flag became the symbol we honor today.

Ancient symbols of loyalty and courage

The exact origin of flags is unknown, but flags have been a part of human culture for centuries. Since ancient times, people have used **symbols** and **totems** to distinguish themselves or their tribe from others. Some groups, such as the Picts, painted or tattooed special designs on their bodies to show what family or clan they came from.

Later people began to make wooden, metal, or stone art objects as symbols of things such as a family or leader or ideas like authority, courage, and religion. Warriors carried **emblems** on the tops of poles to use in battle to signal the location of their leader and to identify friends from enemies. Chieftains celebrated victories by raising their totems over their conquered enemy's camp.

As time went on, symbols became more sophisticated. The Roman army used many different emblems to identify individual units of soldiers. The typical Roman flag had multiple medals and badges with images of animals, laurel wreaths, and portraits of leaders. Flags were raised outside of generals' tents to signal the troops to get ready to fight. Once the battle began, flags were waved to communicate orders.

What do you study?

Until the 1960s there was no official word for the field of knowledge about flags. In 1959, Whitney Smith created a word by combining the Latin word *vexillum*, which means "flag," with the Greek word-ending *–ology* , meaning "the study of." By 1965 his new word, ***vexillology*** (vek'se-lol'e-je), was listed in the dictionary and is now the term for what vexillologists do—study flags. Whitney Smith later became the director of The Flag Research Center in Winchester, Massachusetts.

This print shows early Chinese silk weaving. The Chinese most likely tied silk to poles creating an early version of a flag.

The Romans invented the **vexillum**, which is considered the first true flag. Nobody is exactly sure where or when a piece of cloth was first tied to a pole and waved. Some historians believe that the idea originated with the Chinese, who had been weaving silk since before 3000 B.C.E. The vexillum was a square cloth, usually red, painted with a figure or saying and hung from a horizontal bar at the top of staff. When Roman legions marched with their vexilla (the plural of vexillum) raised high above their heads, opposing armies knew exactly who was coming their way.

Generals knew that the flags were powerful symbols. For soldiers the vexilla meant courage and loyalty, and a point to rally around when the battle got tough.

Red, white, and blue: The king's colors

During the Middle Ages (500–1500 C.E.), flags were used as a rallying point for soldiers on foot and on horseback. Some flags were so big they had to be dragged on to the field in carts. A group of the best soldiers surrounded the cart to guard the flag.

During the crusades, Christian soldiers fought to take control of Palestine and other holy places from Muslims. Soldiers in the crusades marched under the flags of individuals or groups. They were not fighting as countries. Kings, knights, religious orders, and some cities assembled armies to fight under their individual banners.

The Christian cross became a **symbol** of unity for crusaders. By sewing colored crosses onto their tunics, soldiers developed an easy system for identifying fellow soldiers on the battlefield. The Scots adopted the cross of St. Andrew, a white diagonal cross on a blue field, or background. The English favored St. George's red cross on a white field. Hundreds of years later, these crosses would play a part in the designs of the British and American flags.

Seen here are the cross of St. Andrew and the cross of St. George. Both emblems became part of the British flag.

The Union Jack

The Union flag is also called the Union Jack. A *jack* is another word for naval ensign or flag. Although it was designed with bright colors, the Union Jack was hard to see from a distance at sea. To make identification of British ships easier, two new naval flags, the British Meteor and the Red Ensign flag came into use. Several designs of the British flags were used in the colonies. Today's British Union Flag has the red cross of St. Patrick included in its design.

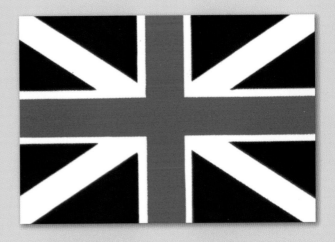

As kings and nobles began to organize larger and more efficient armies, individual regiments designed their own flags, called colors, using the coats of arms of their leaders. At sea, flags were needed for communication. Merchants printed sheets with drawings of all the known flags. Officials consulted these flag sheets to identify ships before allowing them to enter their harbors. Although the flags represented the kings and nobles, people generally associated them with their countries, as well. In warfare, flags became important symbols to be captured or defended.

In 1606 King James I joined England and Scotland into one kingdom. To show that the two countries were united, he combined England's cross of St. George with Scotland's St. Andrew's cross. The Union Flag, also known as the King's Colors, was originally meant to be only a naval flag. However, in 1707 the red, white, and blue Union flag became the king's official royal flag on both land and sea.

Symbols of trouble

About 1000 C.E., the Vikings brought the first flag to North America. The Viking flag, a raven on a white background, was most likely the personal banner of Erik the Red or his son Leif. About 500 years later, flags from Spain, England, France, Holland, and Sweden followed. These flags were not just the flags of kings. Trading companies such as the East India Company also sent their flags to the New World.

Although the colonies eventually came under England's rule, early on they developed a strong sense of independence. By the 1700s, in addition to English flags, colonists flew flags of their own designs. A white flag with a black beaver on it was flown on New York merchant trading ships, and the pine tree was commonly used in various flags in New England. As frustration with the king grew, the colonists adapted the

This early flag is similar to the Culpepper flag or U.S. Navy Jack. It features a rattlesnake with the warning "Don't Tread on Me."

designs of their flags to show how they felt about the English ruler. When the Revolutionary War began, many rebels fought under homemade flags.

The rattlesnake was a favorite **symbol** in the colonies. The Culpepper flag was named after the volunteer soldiers of Culpeper County, Virginia. This flag had not only the snake and "Don't Tread on Me" saying, but also the words "Liberty or Death" and the name of the troop, the Culpeper Minute Men.

Its rattlesnake design came from what many consider America's first political cartoon. In 1754 Benjamin Franklin published a drawing of rattlesnake cut into pieces with the caption "Join, or Die" underneath. Ten or eleven years later, a Massachusetts newspaper published the cartoon in a protest against the **Stamp Act**. Over time the rattlesnake became a popular symbol of national unity against the British.

The Sons of Liberty Flag is considered by some to be the inspiration for the stripes on our current flag. This banner had thirteen alternating red and white stripes. The Sons of Liberty, a **patriotic** society that formed in 1765, protested many British actions in the years before the Revolutionary War.

The flag of the American people

On January 1, 1776, George Washington ordered that the Continental Colors be raised over Prospect Hill in clear view of the British army in nearby Boston. The new flag confused some of the British soldiers. The flag had the British Union Jack design in its **canton**, or top inner quarter. Some British soldiers took this as a sign that the Continental Army wanted to surrender. But others had no problem understanding what the flag meant. The new flag's red and white stripes were the **symbol** of the Sons of Liberty.

The Continental Colors owed much to the Union Jack. They are similar in their red, white, and blue designs. Despite the colonists' anger with England, the Continental Colors showed that the colonies still felt close ties with their former country. However, the signing of the Declaration of Independence showed that the new nation needed a flag that was uniquely American.

Betsy Ross and the flag

A favorite story says that in June 1776, George Washington went to Betsy Ross's upholstery shop in Philadelphia, Pennsylvania, to ask her to make a flag for the new country. When he gave Ross a rough sketch, she suggested that the flag's six-pointed stars be changed to five-pointed ones, because they would be easier to cut out.

There is no definite proof that Washington ever met with Betsy Ross. Ross's family claimed she often spoke of making the flag. However, Francis Hopkinson, a signer of the Declaration of Independence, probably designed the first official flag with the help of a committee. It is likely that they started with the unofficial Continental flag as the basis of the design. It is true that Betsy Ross did make flags. Her design is an example of one of the many variations that were made. It remains very popular today.

This is the Great or Grand Union Flag raised in Cambridge, Massachusetts in January, 1776.

The first national flag

On June 14, 1777, the Continental Congress passed the First Flag Act, declaring that "the flag of the thirteen United States be thirteen stripes, alternate red and white; that the union be thirteen stars, white in a blue field, representing a new constellation." The Flag Act did not determine how the stars and stripes should be arranged. Size and shape were also not assigned.

Flag makers, both professionals and everyday **patriots**, got to work. Each sewed banners with stars and red and white stripes but designs differed widely. Some flags had the stars in rows, others had them in circles. The stripes also varied, although it soon became clear that beginning and ending with the red stripes made the flag much easier to see from a distance.

The variations did not matter. The stars and stripes, used mostly on ships and forts, quickly became recognized as the flag of the United States. Many **vexillologists** consider this flag as the first truly national flag in history. It did not represent a king, a religion, or a trading company. It was the flag of the people of the United States.

Chapter Two: Rockets' Red Glare

Changes in the size of the nation brought changes to the flag. The Second Flag Act of 1794 added two stars and two stripes for the new states of Vermont and Kentucky. This flag, with five rows of three stars and fifteen stripes, inspired a poem that changed how Americans thought about their flag. The flag later was changed back to having only thirteen stripes.

On June 18, 1812, the United States declared war on Great Britain. The war was a result of several long-term quarrels between the two countries. On September 13, 1814, the British attacked Fort McHenry in Baltimore Harbor. The bombing lasted all day and most of the night. Despite the 25 hours of heavy shelling, however, the commander of the fort, George Armistead, refused to surrender. The bombing was so fierce it seemed that the British would capture the harbor; however, the morning after the assault, the American flag was still flying over the fort.

Frances Scott Key, standing on a British ship 8 miles (13 kilometers) from the fort, witnessed the incredible sight. He pulled out a piece of paper and began writing verses of what would become "The Star-Spangled Banner." Key's poem was set to music, and became very popular. The song eventually became our national anthem.

Some people questioned how Key was able to see the flag from so far away. Historical detective work resulted in an interesting theory. When Armistead took command of the fort, he asked that a flag be made so large that the British "would have no trouble seeing it." Mary Pickersgill and her daughter Caroline, assisted by her nieces, a servant, and a slave, worked six weeks to sew the flag. It was enormous—30 by 42 feet (9 by 13 meters). Each star measured about two feet (0.6 meters) across.

The flag was so big that some think the huge flag was not the one that flew over the fort during the bombing. It was too valuable to risk being damaged. Instead a smaller flag was raised during the attack. When the shelling stopped, the flag was lowered. The great flag was then **hoisted** on a 90-foot (27-meter) pole. This theory is

Francis Scott Key observing Fort McHenry. The flag Key saw is on page 14 of this book.

supported in the journal of a British officer who wrote that, as his ship sailed away, he saw the Americans "hoist a most superb and splendid ensign on their battery." Another theory holds that both the large and the small flag were flown during the attack. By all accounts, it is accepted that the great flag was the one that Key saw in "the dawn's early light" and that inspired his words for "The Star-Spangled Banner."

The flag was still there

Before the War of 1812, the eagle, the liberty cap, Lady Liberty, and images of George Washington were favorite patriotic **symbols** in the United States. The flag was recognized as the national flag but it was rarely seen in private homes. "The Star-Spangled Banner" changed all that.

The poem was set to a popular tune and had special appeal because of its words. It told the dramatic story of the battle for the fort—the flag had withstood the "perilous fight." People were proud that, like the flag, they had survived the war. **Democracy** was here to stay. The song declared the United States the "land of the free" and the "home of the brave."

These stirring words changed how Americans felt about their national **emblem**. They began to look at the flag as more than a national flag. They began to see it as representing the character of the people themselves—their ideals and hopes. Americans began to see those "broad stripes and bright stars" as a way to express their own ideas and feelings of what democracy meant.

A symbol of unity

In March of 1861, at the start of the Civil War, Southerners adopted a flag to represent the Confederate States of America. Just as the Continental Colors had resembled the Union Jack, the new confederate flag was similar to the American flag. Despite their desire to break away from the United States, many Southerners still considered the Stars and Stripes to be part of their national heritage.

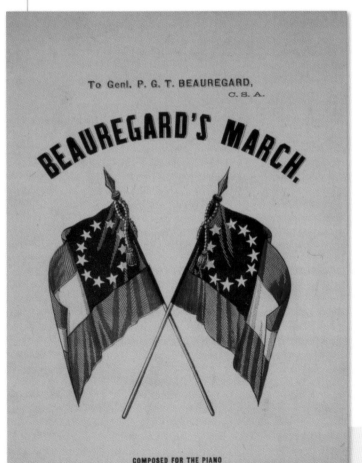

To Genl. P. G. T. BEAUREGARD, C.S.A.

BEAUREGARD'S MARCH.

COMPOSED FOR THE PIANO
BY
CHAS. LENSCHOW.

PUBLISHED BY MILLER & BEACHAM, BALTIMORE.

Entered according to Act of Congress, A. D. 1861, by MILLER & BEACHAM, in Clerk's Office of the Dist. Court of Md.

Many Northerners wanted to subtract stars from the flag for the states that had **seceded**, but President Lincoln refused to remove the stars. The Stars and Stripes, with 34 stars intact, was carried into battle by the Northern army. Throughout the war, the flag remained the **emblem** of national unity.

The flag also played an important role in recruiting men for the army. A Chicago

This Civil War era sheet music shows one version of the Confederate flag. This is not the Southern Cross battle flag that remains controversial today.

songwriter captured the Union's passionate antislavery feeling and linked it to the age-old military command to "rally round the flag, boys . . . shouting the battle cry of freedom." The song became a favorite military march among foot soldiers in the North.

In Northern states, manufacturers could not keep up with the demand for flags. The flag was raised over forts, ships, church spires, colleges, and hotels. It was hung from balconies and displayed on storefronts. Women wore miniature flags in their bonnets and used its colors in the fabric of their dresses. Thousands of soldiers carried small flags with them into battle.

After the Civil War, many thought the North and South would never forgive each other. In 1867 Gilbert Bates, a war veteran from Wisconsin, decided to march 1,400 miles (2,253 kilometers) across the South carrying the American Flag. Starting in Vicksburg, Mississippi, he walked for three months until he reached Washington, D.C. Bates wanted to show that the American flag could once again be the flag of all the nation's people.

Different meanings for different people

The Confederate battle flag, or Southern Cross, remains popular for some people. Some Southerners display the flag on their homes, cars, and clothing as a **symbol** of Southern pride. But for many people, the Southern Cross represents racism and hatred. They see the flag as a reminder of the painful past. Mississippi has the Southern Cross as part of its state flag. In 2003 Georgia redesigned its state flag to remove the symbol. The strong feelings people have about the Southern Cross show how powerful a symbol like a flag can be.

Chapter Three: Flag of the Free and the Brave

Displaying and carrying the flag is an important part of many American holidays. On Memorial Day, people place flags at the graves of war veterans. On the Fourth of July, people carry flags in parades. The flag also has its own holiday.

The first Flag Day is believed to have been celebrated in Hartford, Connecticut, in 1861. The first officially recorded Flag Day celebration was in 1877. In the 1880s, teachers in various states began organizing activities for their student to celebrate the flag's birthday. The idea began to spread, and more and more school districts began recognizing the day as a special event.

At a Flag Day celebration in 1914, Secretary of the Interior Franklin Lane said of the flag, "I am what you make me; nothing more. I swing before your eyes as a bright gleam of color, a **symbol** of yourself." Two years later, President Woodrow Wilson officially established Flag Day as a holiday. After Wilson's proclamation, many communities began celebrating Flag Day. However, it was not until

1949 that President Harry Truman signed an Act of Congress making June 14 a national holiday: Flag Day.

Native Americans and the flag

Although some Native American tribes made and carried flags, many did not. The American flag came to have special significance to some groups as a **symbol** of the land in which they lived.

George Washington believed that the United States should negotiate with Indian tribes in the same way that it did with other nations, through diplomacy. In the early years of the **Republic**, the government sent flags as gifts of friendship to tribal chiefs. The flags featured red and white stripes and an eagle, a powerful Native American symbol, on a blue **canton**.

During the War of 1812, the government refused Native Americans' offers to help in the fight, but one Ottawa chief would not be turned down. Negwagon, who lived in what is now Michigan, declared himself for the Americans and **hoisted** the flag over his camp.

This photograph shows the flag of the Blackfeet Nation next to the U.S. flag.

One day while alone in camp, British soldiers arrived and demanded that he take down the flag. Negwagon obeyed, but then he wrapped the flag around his arm. Raising his tomahawk, he proclaimed that he had "one flag and one heart. If you take one you shall take the other!" Negwagon's war cry brought his braves running back to camp. The British, surrounded by the braves, quickly decided to leave in peace. After the war, Negwagon traveled with his family to Detroit every year in two large canoes. On the stern of each canoe he proudly flew the American Flag.

As white settlers moved west, treaties with Native Americans were broken and Native Americans were pushed from their lands. By the 1860s, war between the U.S. Army and the Plains Indians had risen to a new level. To show their success in battle, Native American warriors began to decorate clothing and other articles with captured American flags.

At other times, tribes would hoist an American flag to show loyalty to the U.S. government. This gesture was not always honored, however. In 1864, Chief Black Kettle flew both a white flag of surrender and an American flag over his camp as a sign of peace. Yet a force of Colorado militiamen ignored the signals and attacked, killing hundreds of Cheyenne and Arapaho.

Today federal law recognizes Native peoples as **sovereign** nations within the United States. Many tribes are designing and adopting official flags of their own as symbols of pride and inspiration.

Respecting the flag

By the late 1800s, people knew the flag triggered strong feelings in most Americans. Some people thought it could be used for many things, including selling everyday products. Manufacturers put the flag on their products and in advertisements to imply that their goods were "all-American." Not everybody thought this was the right thing to do. Some people thought the flag should be handled only in a very formal way—with great care and respect. The issue was taken to court. In 1900 the Supreme Court of Illinois ruled that a merchandise label featuring a flag design was not disrespectful to the flag.

On June 14, 1923, the National Flag Conference drafted the Flag Code to provide guidelines for displaying the flag. However, this did not settle all

This advertisement from the 1880s uses the flag to sell sewing thread.

issues relating to the flag. Over the last century many more situations have called into question what is the proper use of the flag.

One dispute arose over the Pledge of Allegiance. Francis Bellamy and James Upham created the Pledge in 1892. In honor of the 400-year anniversary of Columbus's arrival in the New World, *Youth's Companion* magazine sponsored a **patriotic** ceremony that included saying the pledge in schools across the country. The pledge caught on with the public and was officially adopted by Congress.

In 1935, a group of children who were Jehovah's Witnesses refused to salute the flag. Jehovah's Witnesses believe that it is wrong to say a pledge to anyone or anything except God. The children were expelled from school and their parents took the case to the court.

The case went to the Supreme Court of the United States. The Court first decided in 1940 that schools had the right to expel a student for refusing to salute the flag. This decision was reversed in 1943. In its reversal, the Court ruled that state and local governments could not require anyone to salute the flag or say the pledge of allegiance. To do so was unconstitutional because it violated the rights of free speech and religion.

Flag burning

People who disagree with American policies occasionally burn the American flag in countries around the world. Because the flag is such a strong and recognizable **symbol** of the United States, burning it shows just how angry people are with the U.S. government.

Occasionally people in the United States also burn the flag. In the past this was sometimes done to protest American actions, such as the war in Vietnam. However, some people burn the flag simply to show that as members of a free society they have the right to do so.

One incident occurred in 1984, during the Republican Party's convention in Dallas. A man named Gregory Lee burned an American flag. A Texas court found Johnson guilty of breaking state law. In 1989 the Supreme Court ruled that the First Amendment protects a person's right to burn the American flag. It also said the Constitution protects the right to express a personal or political idea even though other people find that view offensive.

In dictatorships around the world, people can be thrown in jail or even executed for showing disrespect to a symbol of the government. Because our laws are founded on the principals of freedom and justice, we have the right to disagree with our country. This means that every citizen has the right to view symbols of America in his or her own way.

This 1979 photograph shows French people protesting the United States' policy in Iran,

"The Star-Spangled Banner" by Francis Scott Key

Oh, say can you see by the dawn's early light
What so proudly we hail'd at the twilight's last gleaming,
Whose broad stripes and bright stars through the perilous fight
O'er the ramparts we watch'd were so gallantly streaming?
And the rockets' red glare, the bombs bursting in air,
Gave proof through the night that our flag was still there.
Oh, say does that star-spangled banner yet wave
O'er the land of the free and the home of the brave?

On the shore dimly seen thro' the mists of the deep,
Where the foe's haughty host in dread silence reposes,
What is that which the breeze, o'er the towering steep,
As it fitfully blows, half conceals, half discloses?
Now it catches the gleam of the morning's first beam,
In full glory reflected now shines on the stream.
'Tis the star-spangled banner, oh, long may it wave
O'er the land of the free and the home of the brave!

And where is that band who so vauntingly swore
That the havoc of war and the battle's confusion
A home and a country should leave us no more?
Their blood has wash'd out their foul footstep's pollution.
No refuge could save the hireling and slave
From the terror of flight or the gloom of the grave,
And the star-spangled banner in triumph doth wave
O'er the land of the free and the home of the brave.

Oh, thus be it ever when freemen shall stand
Between their lov'd home and the war's desolation!
Blest with vict'ry and peace may the heav'n-rescued land
Praise the power that hath made and preserv'd us a nation
Then conquer we must, when our cause it is just,
And this be our motto, "In God is our Trust,"
And the star-spangled banner in triumph shall wave
O'er the land of the free and the home of the brave.

Timeline

1776	Grand Union Flag is flown over Prospect Hill in Boston, signaling American independence to British troops
1777	First Flag Act passed on June 14. Congress adopted the first flag. The Stars and Stripes are first displayed by John Paul Jones in command of the USS Ranger.
1783	Stars and Stripes recognized as the flag of the United States
1794	Second Flag Act is passed January 13. Two stars and two stripes were added to the flag: one for Kentucky and one for Vermont. This is the flag that was carried in the War of 1812
1814	"The Star-Spangled Banner" is written
1861–1865	Civil War
1892	First version of Pledge of Allegiance is written
1923	Flag Code written
1949	President Truman signs a bill making June 14 Flag Day
1960	The 50-star American Flag is unveiled
1969	American Flag planted on the Moon by Neil Armstrong and Edwin Aldrin
1983	World's largest flag flown in honor of Flag Day
2001	September 11, flag hoisted at World Trade Center site to symbolize endurance after terrorist attack

Further Information

The Federal Flag Code lays out rules for how the American flag should be treated. Some of the rules are:

- The flag should only be displayed during the day, unless it is properly lit at night.
- The flag should not be displayed in bad weather, unless it is an all-weather flag.
- The flag should not be draped over the hood, top, back, or sides of a car.
- No other flag should be displayed above the United States flag.

For a copy of the U.S. Flag Code, send a written request to:

Superintendent of Documents
U.S. Government Printing Office
P.O. Box 371954
Pittsburgh, PA 15250-7954

Further Reading

Crewe, Sabrina. *The Writing of the Star-Spangled Banner*. Milwaukee: Gareth Stevens, 2004.

Marcovitz, Hal and Joseph Ferry. *The American Flag*. Broomall, Penn.: Mason Crest, 2002.

Thomson, Sarah L. *Stars and Stripes: The Story of the American Flag*. New York: HarperCollins, 2003.

Glossary

canton top inner quarter of a flag

democracy government in which people represent themselves by voting

emblem object or artwork that represents something else

hoist to raise into position

patriot one who shows love for and pride in his or her country

patriotic showing a love of one's country

republic country ruled by voting

secede to formally pull out of or withdraw from a group

sovereign having supreme authority over a state or nation

Stamp Act law passed by the British in 1765 that required the people in the American colonies to pay a tax for printing legal papers, pamphlets, newspapers, cards, books, and licenses

symbol something that represents something else

totem animal, plant, or natural object used as an emblem for a clan or tribe

vexillology study of flags

vexillum Latin word for the square flag of the Ancient Romans

Index